My L Words

Consultants

Ashley Bishop, Ed.D.
Sue Bishop, M.E.D.

Publishing Credits

Dona Herweck Rice, *Editor-in-Chief*

Robin Erickson, *Production Director*

Lee Aucoin, *Creative Director*

Sharon Coan, *Project Manager*

Jamey Acosta, *Editor*

Rachelle Cracchiolo, M.A.Ed., *Publisher*

Image Credits

cover Oleg_Mit/Shutterstock; p.2 Viorel Sima/Shutterstock; p.3 Andy Z/Shutterstock; p.4 Eric Isselée/Shutterstock; p.5 ifong/Shutterstock; p.6 Oleg_Mit/Shutterstock; p.7 Albert Campbell/Shutterstock; p.8 Beata Becla/Shutterstock; p.9 Hintau Aliaksei/Shutterstock; p.10 Eric Isselée/Shutterstock; back cover Beata Becla/Shutterstock

Teacher Created Materials

5301 Oceanus Drive
Huntington Beach, CA 92649-1030
http://www.tcmpub.com

ISBN 978-1-4333-2554-0
© 2012 Teacher Created Materials, Inc.

I see a **l**amp.

I see a lake.

I see a lamb.

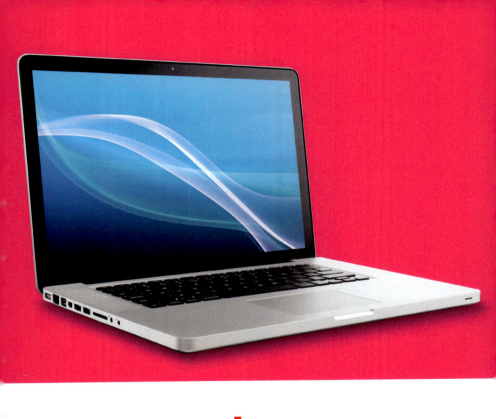

I see a laptop.

I see a lizard.

I see a **l**etter.

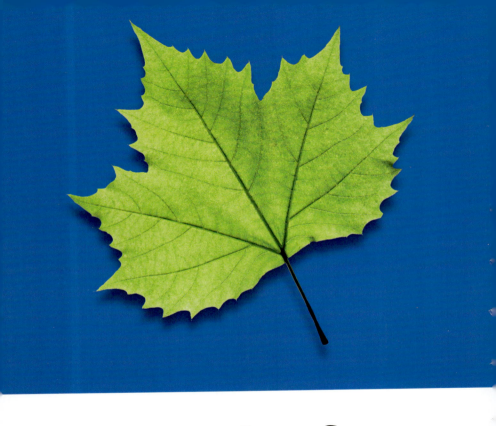

I see a leaf.

I see a lemon.

I see a lion.

Glossary

lake	lamb	lamp
laptop	letter	leaf
lemon	lion	lizard

Sight Words

I   see   a

Activities

- Read the book aloud to your child, pointing to the *l* words as you say them. After reading each page, ask, "What do you see?"

- Discuss the qualities of a lion and a lamb with your child. Remind him or her that the words *lion* and *lamb* begin with *l*.

- Make paper plate faces of a lion and a lamb with your child. You can use cotton balls to decorate the lamb face.

- Have your child dictate a letter to one of his or her friends as you write it.

- Help your child think of a personally valuable word to represent the letter *l*, such as *love*.